CW00507091

West North East

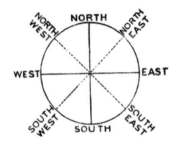

For Kate

I wanted to send a copy
to everyone who'd helped.
Good luck with the 'new phase'
when it comes —

Matthew Clegg
2014

West North East

Matthew Clegg

Longbarrow Press

Published in 2013 by
Longbarrow Press
76 Holme Lane
Sheffield
S6 4JW

www.longbarrowpress.com

Printed by T.J. International Ltd,
Padstow, Cornwall

ISBN 978-1-906175-20-7

First edition

Contents

Raw Poem in Smooth Room

Raw turns up fifteen minutes early
and sweats alone. He labours at casual,
sits on an itch. This doesn't scam easy.
He worries dirt from his nails. Scours the wall
for scuffs. Smooth turns arrive in cliques.
They seat themselves just far enough away
from Raw. They can cuddle in. Steel their backs
by slow degrees. They manage what they say.

Lippy Raw blathers. He curls in his tail.
There's a hornet inside his face. It stings
when Raw flexes his own monkey smile.
Raw wants more know, more easy. He sings
his wish but the hornet twitches and crawls.
Words desert him in search of smoother things.

Fugue

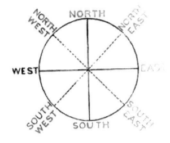

Fugue   1. *Music* > a contrapuntal composition in which a
short melody or phrase [the subject] is introduced by one
part and successively taken up by others and developed by
interweaving the parts.   2. *Psychiatry* > a state or period
of loss of awareness of one's identity, often coupled with
flight from one's usual environment, associated with certain
forms of hysteria and epilepsy.   ORIGIN late 16th cent: from
French, or from Italian *fuga* 'flight', related to *fugere* 'flee'.

The New Oxford Dictionary of English (OUP, 1998)

Because I Was Nobody

Mum's new bloke called me 'the blob'.
I'd no idea what I wanted to do
with my life. I'd come home from job club
and watch anything on TV. It's true,
at dusk I'd walk out of the estate
into the scraggy grazing land beyond
and light fires. On a hump of earth I'd sit
sipping Thunderbird and warming my hands
as lights in the distant high-rise blinked on
and off. Once, I stumbled down a mound
into a herd of cows. The heat of them
was like a drug. All I wanted was to stand
feeling their breath all night. They let me try
because they knew I had nothing. Was nobody.

Fishing by the Trunk Road

My pulse rocked the couch. I had the shakes.
Each binge left deeper bruises in my head
and the kids above could break up a road
with their bass. Stop drinking, for both our sakes
Sandra begged me, and I could see her point.
I'm too hot. Where can a man find quiet?
I knew full well. Round the back of the estate,
behind the new-builds, I could start my treatment.

There's a private pond and the trees – the trees
form a green cocoon around the water.
Peace bunches up in the boughs. I've sat there
long after dusk, alone, feeling my pulse
travel down the rod and line. It stirs up the fish
from the calm; lets heat ebb out of my flesh.

Blood and Ice Cream

Man, it started to go pear-shaped
            for me when Hannah, my first wife,
started shagging my best mate, Matt,
            in the back of his Ford Transit.
The truth is, I married Hannah
            too soon after me and Fay messed up.
Fay rebounded to Matt – who was
            himself holding out for Hannah.
If you've any questions, now would
            be the time to get them asked.
Well, Fay told me that when Matt found
            out Hannah was seeing me
he stopped leaving the house for days
            on end; spent most of his time
with the curtains closed watching
            DVD box sets on a loop:
*Twin Peaks, Edge of Darkness, Buffy
            the Vampire Slayer (Series 4).*
That's when Fay started to take an
            interest in Matt's state of mind.
'You've got to start putting yourself
            about again', she was telling him,
and it looks like he wasted no
            time putting himself into her.
When I got wind of it, all the
            CDs from my time with Fay
started jumping and sticking and
            I couldn't polish them back.
I was rat-arsed on most nights and
            started wasting my hard-earned

on hair restorers that made no
                difference to the state of my thatch.
You couldn't really talk to me,
                I was so welled up with beer.
Is it any wonder Hannah drifted
                towards Matt – the new Matt?
One night I cracked myself wide open
                to some mates in the pub –
finally letting the yolk spill
                that I was still in love with Fay –
that I should climb off my backside,
                go round there and get on my knees.
I took the straight road between Vickers
                and the ice cream factory
and that's when I got jumped on by
                this pair of teenage druggies.
Well, one of the numpties gets lucky
                and twats me full on the nose
whilst the other hangs round my neck
                like a monkey screaming
'Give us your fucking money',
                over and over and over.
Something just clicks and a payload
                of adrenalin whacks my blood;
all this angry-man shit starts
                boiling and foaming up in me
and I'm punching Sunday bells out of
                their pale, pimply faces
until they lose their bottle and run.
                I'm standing there panting,
tooth-marks on my fists; the smell of
                blood and ice-cream in my nose
and hot tears stinging in my cuts. Man,
                I've never felt so pumped.

Spiked

i.

I passed out on some bricks down an alley;
woke up freezing, no clue where I was,
or how to get back to that party –
to my coat, my house keys, my cash.
I remember taking the joint, the head-spin,
the hallway slowly capsizing before
I sprayed the walls with all I'd eaten.
I bailed out of that house and slammed the door –
on what? I hardly knew anyone there,
might never face them again. I'd only
gone for Neil, who fancied the host. Unfair –
I liked her too. A lot. So there I was –
Robinson Crusoe washed up in the city –
weighing these facts, situation hopeless.

ii.

I shivered in the dark like a kitten
fished out of a canal. I had to fight
long and hard with myself not to cry out
or bang on doors. Heavy clouds blew in
smothering the moon. A car braked hard:
I heard a drunk puking up his guts
as if they were his sins, or the city's,
then someone singing *My Way*, every word.
The cast of thousands had shrunk back
to this bitter essence, or its credo.
How long had I lain on those bricks –
fair game for rats and interloping foxes?
I chased down every voice. Not Crusoe:
Caliban, on his island of noises.

iii.

The left hive of my brain asleep, or dead,
half of my face accusing the other –
I thought of Neil. Disguised as a friend, I'd hid
designs of my own, shirking desire.
Life. What steel did I lack to face it?
I walked street after street, utterly uncertain,
even in my pulse. Then I took a right;
heard Neil and our host calling my name.
The trip-hop had flagged and I'd not returned
so they'd started a search. I might even claim
I'd brought them together. Then she took my hand
and my hand let her. Of course she knew
that skunk was spiked with something mean.
She laughed and said it left her kaylied too.

The Last Workday Before Christmas

i.

They'd had me facing flak from angry suppliers
wanting final payments before the Christmas break.
The policy round here was make the bastards wait
then wait some more – until you broke their trust for good.
Phone call after phone call was leaving me uptight –
that's why I locked my desk and binned my party hat
and blew my final afternoon in The Turk's Head.
Alone made perfect sense. I drank another toast
to liquidation soon.

           A young guy in a suit
flirted with the staff: he bought everyone a round
and his smile was sunlight off stacked corporate windows –
blinding. I could see him with my job, fast-tracking
through jammed figures in dodgy books – a magician
disco-dancing through the Great Wall of China.
I downed three flat pints, each with a whisky chaser
before I bristled through the crowds to the station.

ii.

On the teeming platform, a woman with your smile
and ballet-dancer's poise had reached out for the arm
of a disembarking student – and he'd waltzed her.
I thought of the scene awaiting me back home – you
sleeping off another binge on the unmade bed;
fresh cigarette burns following an artery.
Once, I thought I'd be the one to make a difference,
but you reinvent your story every day. Love,
I've no idea what I'm supposed to bring you now.
As the motion gripped and quickened, I let its weight
press me in my seat; imagined the train a shuttle
ascending into the violet smoke that drifted
from the brewery.

        When I slumped off at Crossgates
frost was icing the grit on the far embankment
like Christmas Past. I spied my teenage self, kicking
and dancing amongst the candy of broken glass
in a bus shelter. Something shifted in my guts,
warping through my breath. It all came home to me then –
a moment like his with no thought of the future.
I fretted my keys and looked back at the city –
skylights angled to catch wafers of falling snow.

The Convalescent

i.

He would dope himself on whisky toddies,
crunching chalky Rennies after each.
He managed to find a cure for the migraines
but turned coy when asked what it was.
He lagged his bedroom window with quilts
but nothing blocked out the barking dog.
He thought about grinding glass into its food.
When the nights turned cold, it howled and cried
like the shrinking heart of the never-been-loved.
The owners seemed walled up against it.
His dignity snapped. He stormed outside, naked,
and under a wincing moon lobbed empty
bottle after bottle over the wall, screaming his hate.
He hurt himself more than he hurt that dog.

ii.

Then finally, he let himself collapse.
After months fearing heart attacks,
embolisms, strokes, he watched snowflakes
drift and settle in the broken copse
outside. He watched and watched. A fallen tree
grew an armour of snow that silvered
as the flakes stopped and light recovered.
Fine twigs trembled against the sky
as a flock of pigeons climbed and settled, then
climbed and settled, over and over.
Trucks shook the earth as they turned the corner.
Say what you like: he would begin again
but smaller, lighter. From this point, now,
flyweight squirrels are leading the way.

Sirens

I'm helping them. I'm going to show the rest
of England what it's doing and to who.
These girls: their bodies are a palimpsest

in flesh; every lesion or infected
scab along their veins. Their scuffed and marred looks
tell us what it means to be inflicted

with an existence way back in the queue
and the nudes I'm taking will make it plain.
Look. This has everything to do with you.

And yes, you can trust me. I used to be
an architect, until my accident.
Fell down some stairs and broke my neck. Monthly

injections to prevent my brittle spine
from calcifying. Sweet *memento mori*.
I live off insurance and to stay sane

I buy and sell antiques, write poetry,
paint. Screw money: I try to linger over
something that gives me pleasure every day.

I'm healing. Got myself an art ethic.
When my marriage packed in, I had a phase
when all I did was hang around the chic

cafes, dating university girls
younger than my daughter. Got this earring –
a hint of gold poking through my curls.

Outsider, but not too camp or fey. Spent
hours getting the lowdown on Kristeva,
hard line views and soft skin. I'm no saint.

I'd be drunk and holding forth with some shite
on how we're visionaries when we love;
without it, carbon with an appetite.

All the while I was emotionally
detached. I won't go into how or why,
but once you've been damaged, and I mean badly,

intimacy isn't the same again.
So it was as much a surprise to me
when these street girls cured me. I try to wean

them off hard drugs, give them somewhere to doss
when their pimps get nasty. If they play up –
screaming or nicking stuff from my neighbours –

I cut off their pocket money sharpish.
Discipline. It works, but only to a point.
It's decades since I've been so tapped for cash.

Let me tell you about my first girl, Yvonne.
I was on my way to the Kelham Island
for a date when I started catching on

to how many of these girls were working
the area. Consider the irony
of picking up shags by signs for 'Grinding'

and 'Head Room'; of going at it under
hoardings marked 'Bolts, Nuts, Screws, Studs' –
scarves of plastic fluttering on barbed wire.

She was stumbling along in front of me,
one heel gone, bottle of booze, slip of skirt
spray-painted to her arse, and as I try

to pass her she's shouting all the time, voice
rough enough to sand a barge, 'D' you want it?
Give us 5 quid. I'm bleeding in these shoes.

Get me a taxi. Get me out of 'ere.'
She was crying all down her face, black streaks
of it, wet and oily. Quite a picture.

I wasn't offering any charity,
not to her. I'd given myself eyestrain
on the computer, the balls of jelly

scrunched and bloodshot in their sockets from all
the close work. I told myself I deserved
a bit of release. But that wasn't all.

My date had stood me up. All by myself
I watched the faces, drinking and flirting,
talking the world back to rights. Soon enough

I was trying to imagine the sort
of scars that girl was notching up. Was it
Zola who put the artist and prostitute

on the same pegging? I can live with that.
We get so smug, so sure that what we have
hasn't come out of someone else's pot

of happiness. Mostly, we go through life,
wax in our ears, chained to our galley stools,
thinking we'll be okay, we'll make it through, if

we play our part in the conspiracy
that everything's for the best, and how
can we change a thing? Well, we'll have to see.

I should be careful. You can only hear
so much damage before you start fighting
the current, telling yourself the speaker

is exaggerating, or more often
than not, making it up for attention.
Reality tweaked to serve the medium.

That's the trouble with words. We're nearly immune.
I much prefer images. If my nudes
don't make it as art, someone will buy them.

The Second Chancers

Most people were unconvinced when Ray
and Mary dropped everything to set up house

in a caravan more than halfway
up the Pennines. They piled rocks and car tyres

on the roof to prevent God's pet wind
gusting it to heaven. That Christmas Eve

Ray found his element as he stormed
down to Powergen and said he'd remove

all their doors from their frames unless they agreed
to connect him. Mary was soon

back in hers when – come spring – she rescued
a starving kitten from a wheelie bin.

She fed it with cream off her little finger
and it grew trusting no one but her.

The Vantage

What do you think you're doing? Charmaine asks
each time I bundle our kid in a sling
and take her out, early, before the trucks
hammer the roads. We leave the estate, walk along
the dual carriageway for a mile or so
then cross the central reservation. Once
we surprised a brace of rabbits where weeds grow
behind a billboard, but never again since.

We're heading for the spot where the road cuts
over the river. We can wait a long time
and often go unrewarded, but it's
worth it for the off-chance of seeing him
slow-step the ebb and flow with such grace.
My kid is going to know what a heron is.

The Python

When May remembered itself at last,
I showed my new bloke and my tiny son
the glasshouse. The smell of night-scented stock
was sweet and overwhelming – the colours –
every variation through purple to blue –
close packed and almost bleeding together.
My neck muscles softened in the heat.
Under dirty glass, the air was heavy
as dope. Rob's mobile rang 3 or 4 times
while we were in there, and Ben faffed and poked
at a jet of steam eking pressure from a valve.
I wanted us to rise to spring like those
geraniums wound tight around pillars,
sinuous and alive and brilliant red.

I held Ben's hand and felt my wrists
prickle as we walked back to the Volvo.
As traffic choked up the roads outside town
it felt like my lungs were filling with black.
Then Ben said, 'Is Daddy not my Daddy now?'
A van pushed out in front of us. My pulse
outran my breath and a python of fear
coiled its squeeze around my belly and chest.
I begged Rob to pull over, though it took
an age to find a safe spot to park.
At a roadworks I slumped out and fainted
into a fug of diesel and boiling tar –
clouds fattening above, brilliant white.

The Death Shift

Driving to the care home for an early shift
a screw started tightening in my chest
then snapped. A power spike ripped through me,
5000 volts – my pulse hammering
a break-beat down the length of my arm.
I had to stop the car. Get out. And run.
Look. That road was steep. I got halfway
before I creased. All became clear.
I had to take steps, break the loop
that would always lead back to this.
At the dead centre of a crossroads
I counted my way back into breath.
Those roads pointed at me like four guns,
but no cars came. I unclenched my fists,
and tried to synchronise my heart
with the gradual shifting of light.
Even the planets will wind down,
imperceptibly, as they circle their star.
Jo will die, Ruth and Sarah and John:
they'll slow through my care and stop.
Stretched across a gap in the hedge
a prone cobweb bungied in the gusts –
the spider holding on by one thread
yanked and stretched in bursts of sun.

This Place is Part of Me

It crackles as rain falls through the power-line,
swears at me through graffiti on the viaduct.

I still can't tell rebirth from slow decline.
Every call box for miles of here is fucked.

While Daddy's down the pub getting beers in,
his kids are out to reinvent misconduct.

Call centres, casinos, Kentucky Fried Chicken:
I accept it's mine, but I can't always want it.

Some nights I press a knife against my skin,
drink a bottle too many and pass out.

The ache of this place runs deeper than reason.
Something dies in me with every sunset,

and every morning walks to work again.
It crackles as rain falls through the power-line.

Open to the Sky

England – my England – amounts to this:
a Hull-bound train stalling by a landfill;
gulls and crows scatter from the rubbish

and delay evolves into total standstill.
This is no more than I deserve, no less.
If I ever dream, the place is unable

to deliver. The big guy opposite
sucks on his Coke, bites deep in his burger.
He unwraps *The Matrix* DVD box set.

His balding fleece is endorsed by NASA.
We live on what we find. Like crows. Like gulls.
The sun ebbs and the landfill loses colour.

Lacking anything else, two teenage girls
take photo after photo of each other.

The Power-line

Like taking a kite for a walk, he'd smile –
Bempton Cliffs to Flamborough, pulling to sea,
climbing the wind, thermal by thermal.
There'd been another bout of *myxi*
and rabbits shivered, puff-eyed and scrawny,
on the paths between fields. I was depressed
to think the headland was so diseased;
caravan parks more and more like factories;
each metre portioned out and numbered.

Our nerves had been jangling and raggedy-raw
and no plan we'd hatched had gone right
for weeks. Martin promised he'd love the boy
whatever was up with him, but I couldn't
help feeling it was a punishment –
the scan revealing all that wasn't good
between us. Believe me, it's a hard path
to bear a child you know will be afflicted
and every day I win and lose my faith.

My sleep was getting worse. Night after night
I dreamed the earth lost its grip on the moon
and the tide locked still. Whales swam to light
where unmanned oilrigs smoked under a sun
that burned and swelled out of all proportion.
Martin thought taking the kite might cure
my mood. He let the coil of string unwind
and I made an effort to smile and stare
as it reached its limit and sliced the wind.

I felt our child kick. Thought of better times.
The tide was high and rough. Men and boys
angled from the cliff-tops – their lines of sight
tracking floats riding on the breakers,
whitecaps butting heads against the rocks.
I couldn't believe what I was seeing
and let Martin walk as I stopped to think,
my eyes transfixed by those rods, casting
and gathering so far beyond the brink.

A double rainbow leaped over Flamborough –
so was it here he slipped and turned the kite
into the power-line? I can't remember.
There's a blank between then and the moment
of finding his fallen body. The kite
was tangled, but still skitting and straining
to get free of the string – a stupid toy
out of place where Martin had all feeling
jolted from him. Always slow to let go,

my love was too wired to everything.
Before the thunderbolt had locked on course
was there time for him to reimagine
a future that would leave him in one piece?
I see the shadow measuring his face:
fresh danger signs on every other post;
the path diverted from subsiding ground.
An anxious mother calling back her kids
as gulls and ravens parted ways inland.

Out Far and In Deep

They cannot look out far.
They cannot look in deep.
But when was that ever a bar
To any watch they keep?

'Neither Out Far Nor In Deep', Robert Frost

New Year again. The lighthouse scanned its beam
across the length and breadth of sea and fields
when he traipsed into my watch. One a.m.
Despite the dark, he took the path on trust,

then had his doubts. Folk think they've taken
the straight route to Thornwick Bay: it's a blow
to find this maze of static caravans
and plywood chalets. He tapped my window

and asked which path from here led to the coast.
Mid-thirties. Little else to pin him to,
apart from being there, when the rest
of Flamborough was still toasting in the new.

When the walker left I cracked a Carling
and watched until he broke into a run.
One bloke more with something lost or lacking
bailing out on the clockwork *Lang Syne*.

I should have talked to him more than I did.
A man after my own heart, we shared
something, but it left nothing to be said;
or so I wanted to think. Then I heard

about the missing person. I wouldn't
like to guess if he was really the one.
Above that fuzz of beard his eyes were wet,
but who could say if it was tears or rain?

The coppers found a little Skoda parked
behind The Dog and Duck. It was unlocked,
but out of fuel. A hairline crack had crept
across the windshield – centre right to left.

A sandwich slicked its mayo on the seat.
There was a shirt (still wrapped) and a diary
waiting to be filled. Nothing else, except
that the floor and seat covers were mouldy

and the road tax was a month out of date.
As yet, the police have no leads, and no
witnesses. He didn't leave any note
for those who must be missing him now.

My man seemed to have a hidden purpose,
if no clear idea how to get it done.
There's been no body brought back by the waves,
so I have a theory about this one:

I see him drawing up to the brink that night,
breakers lashing salt against the cliff.
The crumbling chalk glowed under starlight
as he brought himself, tired and frozen-stiff

to face whatever's out there and, alone,
let something go. What we are isn't much,
but it can still tip you over. My man
was heading where none of us can watch.

The Walking Cure

Do you wake up tired and stoke your flagging drive
with mugs of coffee silted strong and black
as you sit blank or doze and start until
the time when you must grind your gears for work?
Then take a hint from me, if only once,
and when the spring tips up its early light
unhitch your conscience, friend, and ring in sick,
and close your ears to that familiar tone
that carps up without pause to make a play
upon your better side. Did that soft gem
win you any wages but more grief?
You know I'm right: so fork out on a map
and hike. At first, no doubt, each step you take
is hampered by the dodgems of the crowd
or traffic jams that load the looping breath
and wind it tight around the sinuses.
Keep pacing long and long in dipping sun
and you'll come slowly into places where
nothing works too hard at winning your
attention. Armed with thought and little else
to keep the growing silences at bay
you'll find yourself near weightless and tuned in
to paths that curve smooth gradients of hills.
And if, before too long, you come alone
and tired to where horizon shows no sign
of what you left behind, you'll stop and hear
a curlew's muted dot-to-dot of sound

and twilight turns the dimmer switch. There
you'll feel a question coming to the brink
and the only answer audible for miles
is oxygen being fed into your brain
by a pulse imploring you to listen.

Edgelands

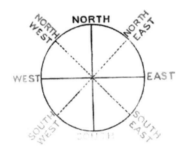

1

To sleep right through until dawn
he must sink a half-bottle
and play Mozart on repeat.
Silverfish scale the duvet
twisted and kicked to the floor.

2

His life is like this: acid
reflux at 4.00 a.m. One
antacid left in the pack.
He chews at it in the dark –
damp, sour, one short of enough.

3

Dawn finds a tissue of cloud
as if space has shed a skin.
Love ends here: a square of light
where jet trails cross and melt,
oh-so-slow, like stitches in flesh.

4

Last night he dreamed a rose –
petals blowing into a skip.
Noon. Time stretches out and holds
like the faraway rumble
filling the valley with its low.

5

As if something is pushing him
to the far edges of life:
this golf ball lodged in his throat;
the sour-bin smell of need, under
his skin, so it won't wash out.

6

He's been too inward-looking.
The slug trail on his window
traces a perfect love knot
before stopping abruptly.
It has a fine pelt of dust.

7

His heart melts when a young mother
unclasps her man's ponytail.
Their two-year-old reaches
up her tiny arms – catches
one split-hair as it floats free.

8

He thought the girl in the park
was kneeling at an easel
where she blended her colours.
No, she crouched at a pushchair,
dabbing the lips of a child.

9

Tab-ends. Cans. Baking dog shit.
Lads on community service
tend the roses of this county:
heavy-headed. Stems unbroken.
And so preternaturally white.

10

He reads too much into this:
on the edge of the playground
a cone of whipped ice cream, dropped
and melting into a puddle
wrinkled by this sudden wind.

11

Scraith Wood path. A shrew, dead –
tail and feet pointing skywards.
A cobweb spun between them
is a pewter cat's cradle.
Hungry flies figure-of-eight.

12

In the derelict car park
he sees poppies poking through:
young men with remote controls
buzz toy cars over petals.
They glare. Screw tab-ends under foot.

13

Edgelands. Showrooms, factories
lapsing into pylon fields.
Where the road bends, fresh debris.
A hubcap like a felled star.
A severed tail. Grey. Still puffed.

14

Opposite the bakery,
a workshop. Smells of muffins
percolate with scorching steel.
In the road, men in visors
cadge lights from men in hairnets.

15

Hagg Hill Lane climbs sharply
on the turn. The inmost edge
is cruelly scarred with welts
and divots. Not like a road,
more some cooled, volcanic flow.

16

Under a dank railway bridge,
he can't make a connection
between a white bra and panties
and an oil-singed workman's glove.
Does he mean can't, or won't?

17

Against the violence of drills,
shunts and clatters, the love song
ghosted from the factory floor
makes him stop, squat in the road,
and add his voice to the tune.

18

On Birley Edge, a bottle
of WKD tossed in the grass –
ice-blue against emerald-green.
He raises it to the light –
counts 6 flies, drowned, ripe, black.

19

Loxley Woods. Time on his hands.
He rests against a poplar,
light strobing into his face:
aphids sketch air currents
all the way up to the sun.

20

In this lonely beer garden
his mind drifts, finds itself
in the trance-world of slow cloud.
Light and dark shift emphasis
across their vast cerebrum.

21

Two paths diverge in a wood –
he takes the one less travelled.
After hacking through brambles
and ferns, it all but peters out.
What next? Check for ticks. Turn back.

22

The setts have nearly collapsed
in the rains. He remembers
two badgers in car headlights –
their rugby-players' shoulders
as they sprinted for the verge.

23

Refuse truck fast approaching –
a worker bee in the grit,
tiny abdomen pumping.
One wing lifeless, the other
straining for purchase on air.

24

Three horses – black, auburn, white.
Black: on its feet, shaking off flies.
Auburn: on its side, head up.
White: flat out, ear to the ground,
listening for its own absence.

25

On Myers Grove Lane
he can't tell if the rushing
in his ears is the river,
the drains under tarmac,
or wind through bunched-up trees.

26

Stacey Bank. A fishing pond
under a power cable.
He watches tattoos jig
on the biceps of fishermen
catapulting wads of bait.

27

In reach from a rising bank,
a frayed nylon rope is hitched
to a pylon's lowest rung.
Boys swing out over nettles,
staring skywards through barbed wire.

28

The Don is a hash of sticks
and broken trees. Buddleia
shake their long, crocodile heads
over fridges, gashed sofas,
4 VDUs, screens smashed in.

29

Low branches over the river.
A scarf of torn fabric
hangs and trails like a dead
heron's wing – elegant, stark;
the colour of ash soaked by rain.

30

These desolate gravel roads
connecting landfills, factories,
are bleached white by midsummer.
Bin bags under sun-kilned mud
clench, obdurate as fossils.

31

In the supermarket car park
an assistant propels a train
of trolleys. One hand off the bar,
he lets them drift in an arc –
a barge on wide-open water.

32

The river is stained with iron.
As the flow licks against a bank
a slow cream of foam conjures
the image of a huge skate
or angelfish, golden brown.

33

Leaves puzzle through stones
over the Rivelin. Here, life
is a single wasp surveying
the rim of a half-sunk can.
A dazzle, spreading and gone.

34

Not all care goes recognised.
Take this sloth-walking old man
who, habitually, places
dropped cans, pop bottles, fag packets
on the tines of railings, gates.

35

Passing the Lexus showroom,
he barely recognises
the reflection in the glass –
an extra in a slightly
speeded-up film. Jerky. Tense.

36

One car towing another.
They must both fix the tow rope
in the lap of their calm.
Let it slacken, then snap tight
too quickly – and it breaks.

37

Pink dusk. Along this B-road
starlings have colonised
20 yards of power-line.
Their song is a kind of current,
the current, a kind of song.

38

Discarded on this vergeside,
a whole car windshield, untinted.
When pressed, a creaking mosaic
of cracks. He imagines the car,
wide open to wind, pollen, rain.

39

Is this his summer harvest?
He finds a lost pair of trousers
from the day he waded the fields.
Unwashed, fallen behind drawers,
the turn-ups filled with barley seeds.

40

All he wanted, once, was her –
the waves in her pastel-red hair,
her perfume, upwind, on the air.
On some purple, faraway moor
to peel a blood orange. Share.

Chinese Lanterns

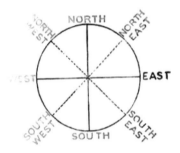

Li Po's Note to Self

I was him once
but I fell out of that boat, drunk,
    and woke up here
where no one will sit next to me.
My voice shakes like someone writing
    on the back seat
of this bus slugging into town.
    We round a bend
and pigeons swat the air in panic:
they are the ash of burnt poems
    spiralling up
and their shadows are threads I've lost.
A clown walks up and down Langsett,
    pushing a pram
to raise pennies to fight cancer.
    He has green hair
and the shot knees of a veteran.
    Last week my Hindoo Doctor barked:
'What is it gone wrong with your face?
    If you have piles,
you must learn ask for your ointment!'
He had the voice of Chairman Mao
    and nurses say
    he cares too much.

Panic in Detroit throbs from a jukebox
and bottles chink at the foot of the weir.
A squad of fans decamps from the sports bar
as one of their own shot-puts a bag of chips
      at a takeaway front.
Another unleashes fists at a man
who collapses like a marionette
      scissored from his paddle.
The down man's lover stands over his head –
the brace of her feet shielding his temples.
Her slender body is all point and glare –
a fighting heron over her fallen mate.

Joni sings *In France They Kiss on Main Street*
        from a plasterer's van;
rhododendrons are icing-sugar pink.
With gym-pumped arms, a bare-chested Ryan
        hoiks Susan from a bench.
Ringed hands around his bull-neck, she flops
        her hair and rolls her eyes
in an *X-Factor* cover of sexual bliss.
She halts in its tracks the stunned jury
        of a single-decked bus.

The cherry trees are creamy with blossom.
There is a woman works Middlewood Road –
       wiry, always hooded.
I first saw her splayed out on the pavement –
her bagful of leaflets spilled at her feet:
       'Come to Spice of Bengal...'
Two litres of White Lightning in her grasp
and a fixed, goblin downturn to her mouth –
she abused me for the distance I kept.
       And now as I look down
from the cappuccino shake of blossom
I see her filch a pasty from a bin
and slot it in her mouth –
massaging the grease into her lips.
       She can't eat the blossom.

Lao Tzu Says

If you don't want people rioting,
don't honour their bankers above them.

To keep them from breaking shop windows,
place less value on things.

If you want them steady and at peace,
market doobries within their budget.

When governing people,
relieve their minds and fill their bellies.

The true man of vision
shields the people from steam-rolling news,
and frees them from wish lists.

He constructs a city
where managers will sit on their hands.

Order will prevail most
following the plan of least action.

This morning Love summoned me in a dream.
Windows and doors are open again in her house.
All the children we never had pour in
      and call us by name.
I climb the purple stairs to her bedroom –
lavender and teasing fingers of light.
She emerges from a cocoon of white sheets
having slept off the hangover of us.
She rises and tilts her breasts to my kiss:
      they are cool and white
as delicately peeled pears. Chinese pears.

The fact is I talk too much when drunk.
Even more when others keep their counsel.
I point out the flaws of eminent poets.
I praise the virtues of those overlooked.
I ought to wake hungover, abashed
      but am given a world
      hand-painted by a child,
      lavish with glitter.
      I sit out and sip tea:
ants scour the fallen helmets of snails;
spiders shrink into the crevices
of clothes pegs hung like sleeping bats.
      I am their poet. Just theirs.

I've offered my advice to the young
    who fly off the handle
as I only jaw myself deeper.
On spinning mornings of aftermath
I've sighed and winced myself bulimic.
    No, I'll not drink again.
Let me shore up in bed for a week
    with the curtains sewn shut.
Test Match Special must commentate rain;
my laptop play itself at Mahjong.

A Letter from Tu Fu

While you sleep off the drink,
high Jumbos score a lattice across blue –
creases to fold origami heaven.

I venture out, alone,
only intending a lap of the park
        but am signalled and fired
        by the tennis of light
volleyed off the mirrors of turning cars.

At Wadsley Bridge I clamber to the edge
        that measures the city
where I stand, level with the power-lines
and feel the skin tighten around my skull.

Below me, 90 feet,
the mangled char of a convertible
has been tumbled off the edge and rests prone
        on the railway tracks
while time pricks like a beak inside an egg.

I count 3 butterflies,
a hovering kestrel,
and the *thee-ewe, thee-ewe*
of some spry, flitting bird.

I would roll up this day
with a sprinkling of coarse black tobacco
for you to smoke out the moths in your head.

Confucius Says

This is why I lose sleep:

when I fail to cultivate virtue –
or won't deepen what it is I've learned.
        When I'm informed what's right
and I squirm from moving to that point.
My own faults have been raised many times
and I've been unable to reform.

        How I can slide downhill!

I'll set my feet firmly on *The Way*:
        virtue is my target
        (and my only bonus).
My work will lunch on benevolence;
I'll take my holidays in the arts.

I won't turn away any student
        who's offered as little
as the price of a meal for his fees –
but I can't open any windows
        to a soul who hasn't
ground their tiny brain in a salt mill
        trying to understand,
        or not spat out their teeth
        making words chase their thought.

Point out the first corner of a square:
if they can't locate the other three,
don't hammer it home a second time.

Moving With Thought

A man who does not move with pain, but moves
With thought...

'Animal Tranquillity and Decay', William Wordsworth

On April mornings
  after soft rain,
the soil will open
  its cask of scent.

The cherry blossom
  is lit by noon
and bees rev engines
  inside the trees.

Is that old soul manning the checkout
Issa? I know those sagging shoulders
and blackened thumbs. They have known better
than packing bags for smirking students.

I know that laugh and sudden banter.
It cracks his mask when wrapping whisky
for an old friend: 'If we're sacked again,
we're only sacked. The cherry blossoms'.

The willow stoops
in April sunlight
* as you did, sweet,*
into our mirror.

* You'd click the switch,*
then comb the iron
* through falling hair,*
loose as the willow's.

A punter leans outside the bookies.
He flicks a fag towards the pavement
where mums wield prams or double buggies
and schoolboys yield into the gutter.

He sighs and waits as if for something
he cannot find the proper noun for.
He cricks his jaw and tongues the craters
where nagging teeth no longer yellow.

I did not know
how trees shed even
 in summer. Now,
the tallest aspen –

 noon's treasurer –
is relinquishing
 one, two, three leaves.
I feel their passing.

By Regent Court boys call him spastic.
They ape his legs that almost buckle
under his weight with every stagger.
The day is hot. He could be dangling

those ailing limbs in the cool Rivelin's
iron-rich chill, not grafting friendless
on heaving streets. Men's fates are cruel.
I buy white wine. I too will stagger.

With this World Cup
streets are as empty
 as bars are full.
Long before twilight

 a faint half-moon
under frail cirrus.
 Swallows and I
make this our city.

[When I'm sober mostly I feel lost,
out of context. A pastiche of me
by a lesser poet. I'm too old
to be saying what he makes me say.

It's not China – and to make things worse
it's not even the right part of town.
I must travel to the London Road
for rice noodles and sweet Oolong tea.]

How many years
are left for walking
from Bradfield, drunk?
How many summers?

From hedge to hedge,
bees tickle foxgloves:
swallows flash white
breasting the suntraps.

Piled in a skip outside the factory
corkscrews of steel shavings catch sunlight.
The steady glare is river silver
lifted from time and flow. It hardens.

In Beeley Wood pan-lids of dazzle
fall on the earth, breaching leaf-shadow.
Not one of them is a perfect circle;
they make the path fidget like water.

I dreamed my skull
became self-storage
and felt a door
slam shut forever

on shoes and clothes
and vinyl albums
and every hair
of mine with colour.

Fill a pint glass with malt whisky –
it looks and tastes like standing urine;
but pour a shot into a tumbler
and you kiss gold and taste a poem.

Paint a wall red, or a whole complex –
it won't catch light, or hold its promise
like the thin stalk of a June poppy
shaking a cup at queuing traffic.

A small child's voice
close at my window:
 'look at that bird,
what is it doing?'

 I cannot see,
but long to answer.
 The voice is high,
clear as a swallow's.

Up from the foot of a cracked drainpipe
a surge of spray is hosing skywards –
tall as a man leaving the sports bar
who belts his song at cloth-eared heaven.

After the storm the concrete pathways
through Hillsborough Park gleam like channels
easing their way through wide estuaries
of silt and sand ferrying moonlight.

From the back seat
of a stretch limo
  a woman's hand
appears to beckon.

  She wears no ring,
no friendship bracelet,
  but harps the air
with languid fingers.

I run to watch a paraglider
losing his hold on sliding thermals:
he comes to hang in the wide branches
of a tall oak until he wriggles

free of his straps. Now he wrestles
in tug of war with a sky dragon
and leaves rain down like birds or fishes
coming to hands he cannot open.

Letter to a Translator

I think of you in this sweltering heat
      in your sun-facing cell,
and how you are not permitted to vent
      about any aspect
of your work or your working conditions
for fear of Diplomatic Incident.
In that hive of four hundred offices
      assignments involving
point by point logs of safety restrictions
and the slow accounts of human torture
exert their equal semantic pressure –
      but, still, you cannot say
what grave matters you are flying across
the Pacific Gulf between languages.
      Should it all prove too much
      may your concentration
wander to recall your one year teaching
in Africa and that some calm Sunday
      you finish your story
      about camel traders
      through the eyes of a girl.
Remember how you told me you were not
the child of a single creed or country.
You said only in the migrations
      between one lexicon
and another do we grow intimate
with how much of life is unsayable.

Were you here today, I would ask you
to speak Somali in your rapid voice;
        tell me the precise word
for how sunlight ignites crystals in sand;
        or how insects jog air
under gob trees touching toes at dusk.

A Trance-Walk with Musõ Soseki

Satori asks us:
if thought, like spilt mercury,
    always takes the path
of least resistance, what then?
Is it ever enlightened?

*

At The Riverside
the city is a galleon
    being hauled out to sea
by the temporal kraken:
pause, whilst you still can.

*

Sirs, please don't brick up
the useless hole in the wall
    or knock down the frame:
let it stand as a jetty
to land or leap into dream.

*

Something was made here
once. Algae slimes down brickwork,
    deep into grouting.
Breathe the stain of oil and spore:
standing water gathers dust.

*

Wells and Richardson,
accountants; breeze block Titan
    likely to endure
the downturn: blue or grey sky
to capital conversion.

*

Pity brother crow,
jilted by the sky – now stiff
    as a burnt journal
for the jealous wind to browse
the secrets he kept from her.

*

Neepsend gas holder's
high pressure main curves and flumes:
 imagine the breath
of a million Tibetan
throat singers searching for pitch.

*

Parkwood finches flit
through chinks in chain-link fencing
 and methane pockets:
their busy lungs are stitching
a filigree of treble.

*

This leaf-corridor
slanting across the hill-slope
 filters North Sheffield
from view: soundwaves are thermals
lifting it into the trees.

*

Badger poltergeists
wake; tunnel up through brick-chaff
and roubles of glass.
They sniff the growling kart track;
borrow razor wire for fangs.

*

The sun-facing leaves
are glowing as if from veins
circulating light:
those in shade witness, not feel,
the rapture of conversion.

*

Often on trance-walks
I can't quite retrace my twists
and turns going back:
my thread could be left or right;
everywhere could be *The Way*.

Passed over for a contract again.
They say it is my lack of qualifications.
They say I have not proven equivalence.
    The woman who told me so
walks to the lift with tired eyes.
I rode down with her once and smiled.
She did not smile. She did not speak.
    I did not exit with her.
I rode back to the top in deep thought,
    then I took the stairs.

Old School Signs On

This place used to be a nightclub –
       Cairo Jack's.
There's more bouncers now it's the dole.
I met this lass here years ago –
danced like hailstones off a bin-lid.
       She hoed out
with this bennie-fuelled magnet,
       and as they
were tripping off for a taxi
       a piss-head
dozed his wagon right into 'em
and smashed up her beautiful hips.

       See that bloke –
he used to break-dance freestyle here –
not in a crew but he was class.
       Bro'! Old School!
       Good to see
someone from a time you can trust.

Li Po at Gateway to Work

This is a long way from White King City –
       its pink tent of clouds.
Curtis says this room stinks like a toilet.
Will someone open a fucking window,
       he can hardly breathe.
Barry is to lead the morning's session.
He asks us to picture the job we want.
We must imagine the road to that job.
On Friday Katy will take us bowling,
       if we all behave.
This is not the way to the East Ranges –
       their high-rising clouds.
       I load Google Earth
and scout out new havens to drink and fish.
I can see two geese bathing by a weir.
They honk away the ducks that inch too close.
Trees reflect water spirits on their leaves,
       which water mirrors.
       Nine more days to go.
       Ninety spec letters.

Aphorisms make me bite my tongue.
I'm bored with Confucius and Lao Tzu.
I'm tired of white rice and jasmine tea.
      I'll get blind drunk
and walk out into the dusk city.
I want streets narrow between terraces
and paths pink with blossom smears.
      No more sober thoughts.
I want to be a Chinese lantern
and carry light through liquorice clouds
steaming above the Bassett's factory.
I want to be a man with tattoos
green and dense as new-sprung leaves.
      A shivering aspen
under moons round as open wells.

The Falconer

For M.G.

When I first heard you at that open mic
you stood brick-solid as a forward prop
      then released short vowels
and glottals to falcon wings and talons
      around our poky snug
where some of us wanted to cheer or stand
and others chuntered over little drinks.

Your signature limped like a wren through snow,
      and the mobile numbers
you gave were always discontinued
      or one digit missing.
I never saw your poems in magazines.

You'd driven down the M1 to perform,
      and after the fifth pint
added 'it's OK, I'm kipping over
      on Robin's sofa-bed.'
You sussed we couldn't bear to hear you say
      your car seat was your cot,
      and once you'd sobered up
you ate a pie and flogged your engine north
      to wing Biology
      to 6th form girls and boys.

      I wonder if they knew
how kestrels roosted in your frontal lobes?
You were never one for self-promotion.

Honeysuckle Blooming in the Wildwood Air

It is an ordinary evening in Hillsborough
and I've been reading Stevens before bed.
The gutters gurgle like a drain of thought

and I am falling asleep to late Dylan
wheezing through his *Highlands* of the mind.
I am dreaming of a second Hillsborough –

Hillsborough as Cathay and Cathay as a town
far above the sheen of Highland lochs
where streams run off from glaciers above

and into whiskies malted from the light.
Here talk is of the real and reimagined
and Stevens is mandarin of mandarins.

When I was young I dreamed of orchestras
that improvised sweet harmonies from thought –
but as I grew the strings and brass fell out.

Now I dream a twat who punched me once
is puffing smoke into a glass harmonica
like Dylan pioneering Chinese rock.

Socrates on the Meadowhall Tram

The old gadfly is dressed in Wednesday strip
      with a basin haircut
      and his grasshopper legs;
an ancient tape-player under his arm.

      He rewinds the tape;
plays *The Sound of Silence* at a volume
that shakes the atoms of our ribs until
      the battery arrests.

      Every face turns away –
and so it floods: the real sound of silence –
      stern to bow of the tram.

I watch him disembark at Cathedral:
      the still-wily Greek
stoops to question the tramlines with his palms:
they reveal how little we understand
      of the chorus humming
forward and back to the ends of the line.

Li Po's Letter to Rumi

So I will owe to my friends this evanescent intercourse.
I will receive from them not what they have but what they are.

'Friendship', Ralph Waldo Emerson

You came unannounced and, if you recall,
brought me goat's cheese and a deep red Merlot,
      neither too fine or cheap.
You sat contented on my one spare chair –
some green plastic crab I'd pulled from a skip –
      and I opened the blinds
      for the moon and starlight
to make my spartan room furbished enough
      to pass for our tavern.
That was when you told me about sohbet
      and how you believed
that one friend must be still for the other
to make the spirit journey to find him.
      I told you, in return,
      my landlocked exile here
was just an old man's way of travelling.
      I remember your words:
      'Let wine be the current
      of the Yangtze gorges,
and love be the meeting of all gorges!'

We spoke in this vein long after midnight,
and then you announced you had to move on.
        Not for me to question;
but when a friend is honest and giving
I always walk with him part of the way:
        give breath to his stories
as I stumble home drunk under the stars.
That night I slept in a climbing hammock
        under a sycamore –
the sky a reservoir of darkest blue.
I slept with my cash about my person
and did not care who might lift it from me.
        When I woke the dewfall
had left five billion small deposits
on the grass-blades and my whiskers alike.
        I don't know where you are
but I sing these thoughts to the moon tonight
and request that she forward them to you.

Marcel Theroux stops me
and asks me to define Wabi Sabi.
This batch will be my only submission.
I will take great pains
to write an Afterword.
It will explain this new 'version' of me –
the next stage in the art of translation.
I saw Confucius in Jobcentre Plus.
I told him I was looking for work
as a Dadaist temp.
Imagine the sound
of no hand clapping.

Notes

Blood and Ice Cream
Set in Crossgates, Leeds. Until the 1990s Vickers was a munitions factory situated directly across from Treats Ice Creams.

Spiked
'Kaylied' is Northern English dialect for 'shit-faced'.

The Last Workday Before Christmas
The Turk's Head was a pub in Leeds City Centre. It has been re-named Ostlers, but 'the old guard' were still using the original name when I left Leeds in 2003.

The Death Shift
The title was given to me by Paul, a care worker for Leeds City Council. The early morning shift is when a care worker is most likely to find one of his charges has passed away.

Edgelands
This sequence predates the book of the same name by Paul Farley and Michael Symmons Roberts.

A Trance-Walk with Musõ Soseki
The first and last poems in this sequence are versions of tanka by Musõ Soseki. The Riverside is a Sheffield pub by the River Don. The galleon is a graffiti collage by Phlegm.

Li Po at Gateway to Work
The Department for Work and Pensions Research Report No. 366 reads: 'Gateway to Work is a two week, full-time training programme which is mandatory for jobseekers that have been claiming Jobseeker's Allowance four weeks after joining Gateway.'

Li Po's Letter to Rumi
Sohbet is a mystical conversation on mystical subjects.

Marcel Theroux stops me...
Wabi Sabi is a Japanese aesthetic philosophy. The speaker is 'Chinese'. The (fictional) conflation is Marcel's, not the author's.

Acknowledgements

Poems have appeared in *Antiphon, Long Poem Magazine, Matter* and *The Sheffield Anthology.*

Several poems in *Fugue* ('Because I Was Nobody', 'Fishing By the Trunk Road', 'The Convalescent', 'The Second Chancers', 'The Vantage', 'This Place is Part of Me', 'Open to the Sky') appeared in *Nobody Sonnets* (Longbarrow Press 2008). The poems have been revised for this collection.

Alternative versions of *Edgelands* have appeared in pamphlet and matchbox formats (Longbarrow Press 2008). The matchbox edition comprises 56 poems, from which 50 were selected for the pamphlet. The poems have been resequenced (and, in some cases, revised) for this collection.

*

I would like to thank the following people for their invaluable support and input: Elizabeth Barrett, Matt Black, Andy Hirst, Chris Jones, S-L Jones, Brian Lewis, Fay Musselwhite, Alistair Noon and Conor O'Callaghan. Thanks also to Simon Heywood, for those Wednesday nights in the Barrack Tavern.

West North East is dedicated to my partner, Ruth Palmer, and to my nieces, Eleanor and Emily Slater.